The Unofficial Guide to the WORLD CUP

Paul Mason

Editor: Sarah Peutrill
Designer: Darren Jordan
Picture researcher: Diana Morris

ISBN: 978 1 4451 5599 9

Printed in Dubai

Franklin Watts
*An imprint of
Hachette Children's Group
Part of Hodder and Stoughton
Carmelite House
50 Victoria Embankment
London EC4Y 0DZ
An Hachette UK Company
www.hachette.co.uk
www.hachettechildrens.co.uk*

Please note: *The statistics in this book were correct at the time of printing, but because of the nature of sport, it cannot be guaranteed that they are now accurate.*

FSC
www.fsc.org

MIX
Paper from responsible sources
FSC® C104740

Picture credits: ABACA Press/PAI: 26b. AGIF/Shutterstock: 23tl. The Asahi Shimbun/via Getty Images: 19tr. Jefferson Bernardes/Shutterstock: 28br. Bettmann/Getty Images: 12t. Gabriel Bouys/AFP/Getty Images: 17tr. Andrew Burton/ Getty Images: 4cl. Cal Sport Media/Alamy: p.22 bl. Enrique Calvoal/Dreamstime: 4cr. catwalker/Shutterstock: 5t, 9b. CP DC Press/Shutterstock: 21br, 22bl. chaofann/istockphoto: 1bg. Donatus Dabravolskas/Shutterstock: 21cr. Ivica Drusany/ Shutterstock: 28t. Empics/PAI: 25b. ph.FAB/Shutterstock: 29m. Ina Fassbender/Anadolu Agency/Getty Images: 17l. Fauzan Fritzia/Shutterstock: 20t.Fitria Ramli/Shutterstock: 20b. Frimu Films/Shutterstock: 28t inset, 28c inset, 29t inset, 29c inset. Alex Grim-FIFA/via Getty Images: 9t, 29b. Haynes Archive/ Popperfoto/Getty Images: 13t. Hulton Archive/Getty Images: 24tr. Marco Iacobucci/Shutterstock: 23br, 29b. ID1974/ Shutterstock: 20bl. kivnl/Shutterstock: p.23 tr. Influential Photography/Shutterstock: 29t. Andrey Kuzmin/Shutterstock: 12b, 21br. Monaliza0024/Shutterstock: 20m. Alexandre Lourerio/Getty Images: 5c. MDI/Shutterstock: p.28c. Juan Mabromata/AFP/Getty Images: 2b, 16. Francois Xavier Marit / AP/PAI: 25t. My Vector/Shutterstock: 29bl inset. Metin Pala/ Anadolu Agency/Getty Images: 4b. Tatiana Popova/Shutterstock: 14c, 20c. Popperfoto/Getty Images: 7b, 8b, 26t, 26c. A Ricardo/Shutterstock: 19bl. Gevorg Ghazaryan/Shutterstock: 28bl. Sanjay JS/Shutterstock: 20b. Antonio Scorza/AFP/Getty Images: 18. Christophe Simon/AFP/Getty Images: 15. Sven Simon/DPA/PAI: 27l. Neil Simpson/EMPICS/PAI: 27t. Patrik Stollarz/AFP/Getty Images: 24b. Laszio Szirtesi/Shutterstock: 10. The Other Final DVD cover/wikimedia commons: 11cl. Bob Thomas/Popperfoto/Getty Images: 6-7. Sion Touhig/Getty Images: 9c. Ulsteinbild/Topfoto: 13b. Roy F Wylam/Shutterstock 20t. Friedmann Vogel/Getty Images: 11r. Every attempt has been made to clear copyright. Should there be any inadvertent omission please apply to the publisher for rectification.*

CONTENTS

Words in **bold** are in the glossary on page 32.

THE BIGGEST SHOW ON EARTH

Imagine if every person in every one of the world's 40 biggest cities* sat down to watch a football match. It would be a big crowd! But the World Cup final is actually watched by TWICE that many people.

*And remember, London and New York aren't even in the top 20.

The World Cup is the only sports event bigger than the Olympic Games. Experts think one in nine of the world's population watch the final. That means about 840,000,000 football fans are likely to be glued to their screens for the next final, on 18 December 2022.

RECORD SETTER!
One of the best World Cup goalkeepers ever is England's Peter Shilton. In three World Cups between 1982 and 1990, Shilton only let in eight goals from **open play**.

RECORD SETTER!

The only player to win three World Cups is Pelé of Brazil. He won the first two in 1958 and 1962. At the 1966 tournament Pelé was so badly fouled by the opposition that he vowed never to go to another World Cup. Fortunately for Brazil, Pelé changed his mind, and they won again in 1970.

CHAMPIONS OF SPORT

1 Rls POSTAGE AJMAN ريال عجمان بريد عجمان

Brazil's Pelé, often said to be the best footballer of all time.

A tough tournament to get to

The World Cup only happens every four years. It features only the world's best teams (see page 10). This means even getting their team into the World Cup is an impossible dream for most countries. And after every failure to get there, the teams have to wait another four years for their next chance.

James Rodriguez of Colombia scores past goalkeeper Fernando Muslera of Uruguay during the 2014 World Cup in Brazil.

A tough tournament to win

If your team DOES make it to the World Cup, the chances of winning it are tiny – especially if you don't happen to be Brazilian, German, Italian or French. By 2018, those four had won 15 of the 21 World Cups so far.*

Even if their own team doesn't make it to the competition or gets knocked out, though, the World Cup still gives fans around the world a whole month of football fun.

*So four countries (just 2 per cent of teams that tried to qualify for Qatar 2022) have won 71 per cent of the World Cups so far.

IT'S A FACT!

The football team from the tiny European country of Luxembourg has been trying to qualify for the World Cup since the second contest in 1934 – but has never managed to get there.

WORLD CUP HISTORY

When Brazil played Uruguay in the World Cup final in 1950, almost 200,000 people crammed into the stadium.* But the World Cup had not always been quite this popular. In 1930, at the first World Cup, only about 300 people watched Romania versus Peru.**

*Officially, 173,850 people bought tickets – but so many others got in without them, the crowd size is said to have been 199,854.
**The smallest crowd ever recorded at a World Cup game.

Olympic roots

The idea for the World Cup came from Olympic football tournaments of 1920–28. The Olympic matches were popular, but only **amateur** players were allowed. This meant that the best players, who were mostly **professionals**, could not take part. **FIFA** decided a new competition was needed. It would be between national teams, and there would be no limits on who could play. The first World Cup would take place in Uruguay in 1930.

An enormous, mainly Brazilian, crowd jammed into the Maracanã Stadium to watch Uruguay beat Brazil in 1950.

IT'S A FACT!

The Romanian team for the 1930 World Cup was picked by the country's football-mad king, Carol II. Not only that, King Carol told each player's employer to give them three months off work on full pay, so that they could go to the tournament.

The Romanians came second in their group. In 1930, only group winners made it to the knockout stages – so Romania went home earlier than they had hoped.

The small club of winners

Between 1930 and 2014, only eight teams won the World Cup. They always came from either South America or Europe. After the 2018 competition, the score between the two continents was South America 9–12 Europe.

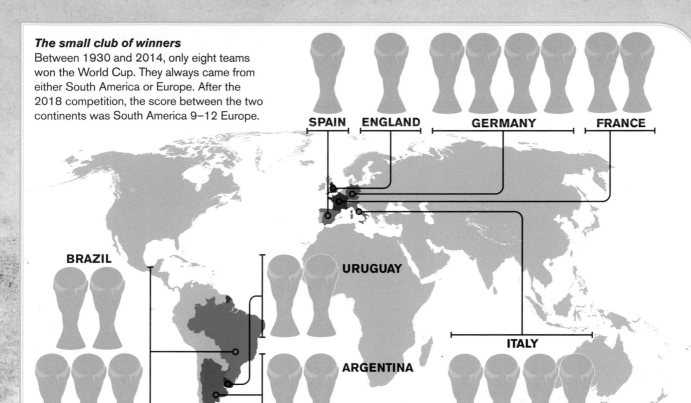

SPAIN **ENGLAND** **GERMANY** **FRANCE**

BRAZIL

URUGUAY

ARGENTINA

ITALY

The first-ever winner was Uruguay in 1930. The government was so pleased, it gave every player a plot of land and a new house in the capital city, Montevideo. Uruguay won again in 1950; the only other teams to have won are Brazil (five times), Germany (four), Italy (four), Argentina (two), France (two), England (one) and Spain (one).

Uruguay, winners in 1930, were the world's best team: they had also won the Olympic football tournaments of 1924 and 1928.

IT'S A FACT!

The original World Cup trophy was called the Jules Rimet Trophy. During the Second World War (1939–45) it was hidden under a bed in a shoebox in Rome, Italy, so that the Nazis couldn't steal it.

In 1983 the Jules Rimet Trophy was stolen from a cabinet in Brazil. It has not been seen since.

TO TEAMS: BRAZIL

Brazil is one team everybody hates having to play at the World Cup.*. Brazil is the only team to have played in every single World Cup so far, and it has won the tournament FIVE times – more than any other team.

*There are two of these. The other is Germany. See page 16 for more about them.

A bad beginning

Although it is now the most successful World Cup team, Brazil got off to a terrible start. In the 1950 final Brazil played Uruguay. The Brazilians were VERY confident of winning. In fact, before the game even kicked off newspapers had been printed saying Brazil had won the World Cup. Unfortunately (if you were Brazilian), Uruguay won the match 2–1.

Brazil was so happy to be hosting the 1950 World Cup, the country built the world's greatest football stadium in preparation: the Maracanã.

RECORD SETTER!
In 1970, Brazil's Jairzinho scored in all six matches his team played – including the final against Italy, which they won 4–1. He is the only player ever to do this.

Style of play

Win or lose, Brazil's style of play is exciting to watch. It relies on the team being full of brilliantly skilful players. Wherever you go in Brazil you see people playing football, on the street, the beach, on basketball courts, in parks … anywhere there's space. That might be why some of the skills and tricks Brazilian players use look more like street soccer than an international football match. The players aim to keep **possession** of the ball as much as possible, and they **dribble** the ball more than usual. They will often run at defenders to try to get past them, instead of passing to a teammate.

Philippe Coutinho of Brazil. In 2016 Coutinho was voted best Brazilian player at any European club (then Liverpool) – beating Neymar to the prize.

Brazil's fans LOVE their team. They're certainly not giving the Germans on the left of this picture a lot of space for their flag!

Big-time winners

After losing to Uruguay in 1950, Brazil soon recovered. Of the four World Cups between 1958 and 1970, the team won three, in 1958, 1962 and 1970. (England won in 1966.) The key player for Brazil during this time was Pelé, the country's most famous footballer. Even when he was not on the pitch himself, Pelé inspired his teammates to play in typical exciting Brazilian style.

Brazil's wins did not stop in 1970: the team also won the World Cup in 1994 and 2002.

Brasil 2002   R$ 0,55

BRASIL PENTACAMPEÃO

1958   1962   1970   1994   2002

Brasil Pentacampeão Mundial de Futebol

BRAZIL'S WORLD CUP RECORD*

Wins	5
Losing finals	2
Semi-finals	4
Appearances	20
Matches played	104
Wins	70
Total goals	221

*up to and including 2014

Left: World Cup fever even affects the world of stamp collecting!

HOW DO YOU GET TO THE WORLD CUP?

If you're a fan, getting to the World Cup is easy. All you need is a month off school or work and a lot of money! For players, getting there is a lot harder.

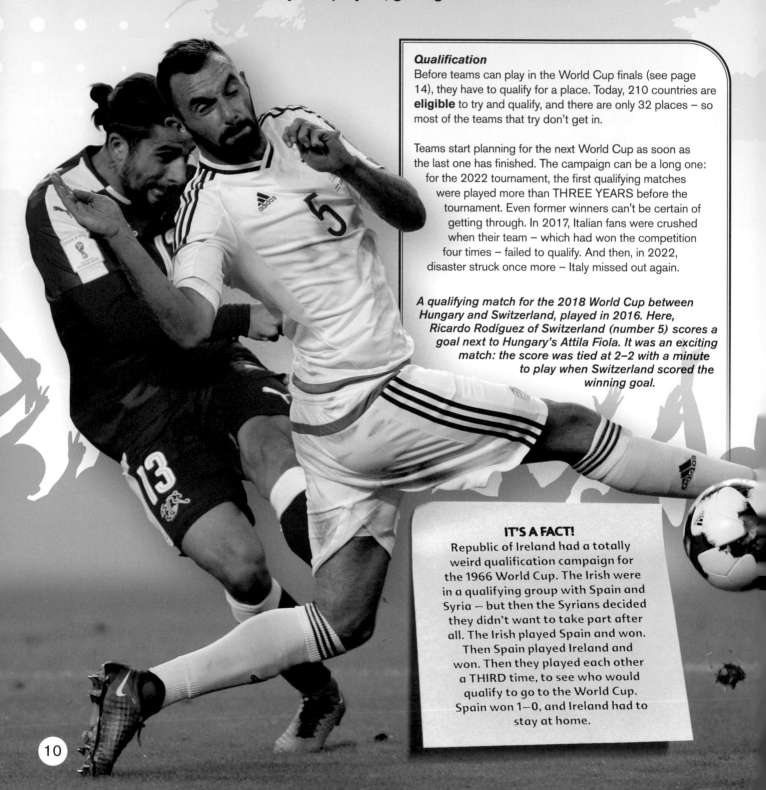

Qualification

Before teams can play in the World Cup finals (see page 14), they have to qualify for a place. Today, 210 countries are **eligible** to try and qualify, and there are only 32 places – so most of the teams that try don't get in.

Teams start planning for the next World Cup as soon as the last one has finished. The campaign can be a long one: for the 2022 tournament, the first qualifying matches were played more than THREE YEARS before the tournament. Even former winners can't be certain of getting through. In 2017, Italian fans were crushed when their team – which had won the competition four times – failed to qualify. And then, in 2022, disaster struck once more – Italy missed out again.

A qualifying match for the 2018 World Cup between Hungary and Switzerland, played in 2016. Here, Ricardo Rodríguez of Switzerland (number 5) scores a goal next to Hungary's Attila Fiola. It was an exciting match: the score was tied at 2–2 with a minute to play when Switzerland scored the winning goal.

IT'S A FACT!
Republic of Ireland had a totally weird qualification campaign for the 1966 World Cup. The Irish were in a qualifying group with Spain and Syria — but then the Syrians decided they didn't want to take part after all. The Irish played Spain and won. Then Spain played Ireland and won. Then they played each other a THIRD time, to see who would qualify to go to the World Cup. Spain won 1–0, and Ireland had to stay at home.

Regional qualification

Around the world, qualification tournaments are organised by region. Each region is allowed a certain number of teams in the final tournament. For 2022, the regions/team numbers were:

⚽ **EUROPE**: 13 places

⚽ **SOUTH AMERICA**: 4.5 places (the country that comes fifth plays the winner of the Oceania region for a place)

⚽ **CONCACAF**: 3.5 places (the fourth-placed team plays the fifth team from Asia for a place)

⚽ **AFRICA**: 5 places

⚽ **ASIA:** 4.5 places (the fifth-placed team plays the fourth team from CONCACAF for a place), plus one for Qatar, the **hosts**

⚽ **OCEANIA**: 0.5 places (the winner plays the fifth team in South America for a place)

The only team that gets in automatically is the host country's. Before 2006, last time's winners also got a pass to the finals, but this does not happen any more.

Jordan take on Uruguay in the 2014 World Cup qualification playoffs between Asia and South America. Uruguay won 5-0 and went to the World Cup.

THE OTHER FINAL

„Ich habe den Film schon dreimal gesehen und bin begeistert!" Zinedine Zidane

"THE OTHER FINAL zeigt den wahren Geist des Fußballs." Roberto Baggio

BHUTAN : MONTSERRAT

IT'S A FACT!
On the same day as the 2002 World Cup final, the world's two worst teams got together to play a match.

The Himalayan country Bhutan (ranked 202nd) played the Caribbean island of Montserrat (ranked 203rd). The cold and altitude of Bhutan made life difficult for the Montserrat team, and Bhutan won 4–0.

WORLD CUP CONTROVERSIES

Most World Cup matches are played in a spirit of fierce but fair competition. Once in a while, though, things do go wrong. Here are some of the best-known World Cup controversies.

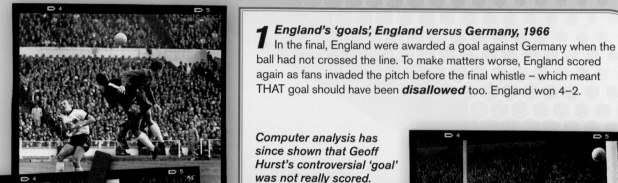

1 ***England's 'goals', England versus Germany, 1966***
In the final, England were awarded a goal against Germany when the ball had not crossed the line. To make matters worse, England scored again as fans invaded the pitch before the final whistle – which meant THAT goal should have been ***disallowed*** too. England won 4–2.

Computer analysis has since shown that Geoff Hurst's controversial 'goal' was not really scored.

2 ***The 'Hand of God', Argentina v England, 1986***
In the quarter-final, Argentina's Diego Maradona scored against England using his hand, rather than his head – but the officials somehow did not notice. Argentina eventually won 2–1, and Maradona said after the game that the goal was, "A little bit the head of Maradona, a little bit the hand of God."

3 ***Šimunić's (eventual) sending off, Australia v Croatia, 2006***
First, Josip Šimunić (of Croatia) got a ***yellow card*** for a too-tough tackle. Then he got another yellow – which should have led to a ***red card***. But for some reason Šimunić wasn't sent off.

At least, not until later, when he shoved the referee after the final whistle had gone.

4 The Battle of Santiago, 1962

At this infamous match between Chile and Italy (left) in Santiago, the first foul took just 12 seconds, and within 13 minutes an Italian player had been sent off. He refused to leave, and had to be taken away by the police. After that there were punches, kicks, elbows and broken noses galore. Amazingly, there was only one further sending off (when an Italian kicked one of the Chilean players in the head). The police had to come onto the pitch three more times to restore order, and Chile eventually won 2–0.

5 Germany and Austria advance, 1982

With an earlier match between Algeria and Chile already finished, Germany and Austria knew that a 1–0 Germany win would get both of them into the knockout stage. Germany scored within 10 minutes of kickoff. Both teams then spent the rest of the match passing the ball harmlessly around. Germany went through, Algeria went home.*

*The tournament rules were changed after this: now, the last matches in each group are always played at the same time.

Germany against Austria at the 1982 World Cup. The organisers were horrified at the two teams' actions, and later changed World Cup rules.

GROUP AND KNOCKOUT STAGES

The month-long World Cup tournament is called the World Cup finals.* The finals are separated into two parts: group stage and knockout stage.

*This is different from the 'World Cup final', which is the match to decide the winner.

Group stage

For the first part of the finals, the teams are organised into groups of four. Each group contains one of the world's top teams, and one that is low ranked. The two other teams are somewhere in between. The specific teams for each group are chosen at random.

The groups are like mini leagues. Each team plays all the others, so play three matches in total. At the end, the top two teams from the group go into the knockout stages.

SCORE

In the group stages, many teams concentrate on not losing. As a result, the matches can be low on goals – but high on tension.

Knockout stage

The knockout stage gets its name because if you lose, you get knocked out of the World Cup.**

Where you finished in your group affects your path to the final, because the winners of one group play the second-placed team from another. In theory, winning your group means your first knockout match will be easier.

The knockout structure is:

Round of 16

↓

Quarter-finals

↓

Semi-finals

↓

Finals or third-place playoff

The most any team has to play is three group-stage matches and four knockout ones. Play seven games, and win all of the last four, and you win the World Cup.

IT'S A FACT!
The 'Group of Death' is the name for a group so filled with strong teams that it will be especially hard to qualify for the knockout stages.

The name was first used in 1970, to describe a group with England (the champions), Brazil (1958 and 1962 winners), **Czechoslovakia** (1962 finalists) and Romania.

2014 World Cup GROUP G

Germany

Portugal

Ghana

United States of America

At the 2014 World Cup, Group G was the 'group of death'. Its top team, Germany, was ranked second in the world. Even the lowest-ranked team, Ghana, was 23rd.

**There is one exception: the losing semi-finalists play a match for third place.

*There were four **penalty shootouts** at the 2014 World Cup; this was the last. It is Argentina versus Netherlands in the semi-final. Argentina win 4–2.*

IT'S A FACT!
The first World Cup match decided by a penalty shootout happened in 1982. It was a semi-final between Germany and France. Inevitably, Germany won. (Between 1982 and 2014, the Germans took part in four penalty shootouts at the World Cup — and never lost one.)

When the groups for the World Cup are announced, one of the first questions rival coaches ask is, "Are we going to have to play Germany?" If the answer is no, they breathe a sigh of relief.

The best World Cup team?

Germany has won the World Cup four times, once fewer than Brazil. Even so, some people think this is the most successful World Cup team in history. It has played in the final eight times (once more than Brazil). It has come third four times (twice as many as Brazil). And in the 20 World Cups played between 1930 and 2014, Germany has finished in the top three 12 times (three more than Brazil).

RECORD SETTER! Germany's Lothar Matthäus has played more games at the World Cup than any other player, with 25. He and Mexico's Antonio Carbajal are tied for the most tournaments played, with five.

2014 FIFA W

FIFA WORLD CUP Brasil

REUS 21

CHAMPION

2014 FIFA World Cup

2014 World Cup semi-final

In the 2014 World Cup semi-final Germany played Brazil, the hosts. They won 7–1, and set all sorts of World Cup records:

- Miroslav Klose scored his 16th World Cup goal, one more than the next best top scorer ever – Ronaldo of Brazil.
- Germany reached their fourth semi-final in a row, which no one else has done.
- They scored the five fastest goals in World Cup history (four were scored in just 400 seconds).
- Germany's goals took their total in World Cup history to 224, two more than Brazil's.

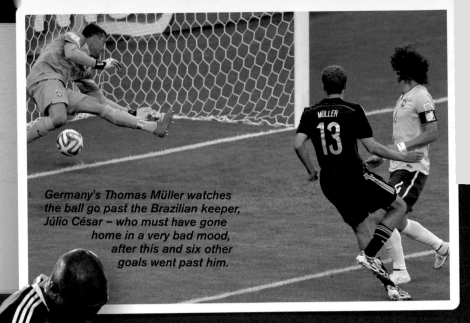

Germany's Thomas Müller watches the ball go past the Brazilian keeper, Júlio César – who must have gone home in a very bad mood, after this and six other goals went past him.

Style of play

Germany play a style of football based on a solid defence. It helps that the goalkeeper, Manuel Neuer (left), is usually said to be the best in the world. The team almost always plays with four defenders and two defensive midfielders, which makes it hard for the opposition to find space close to Germany's goal.

When the midfielders get the ball in defence, they often play long, accurate passes to the forwards. Defence suddenly becomes attack, which is why the team scores a lot of fast goals on the ***break***.

RECORD SETTER!
Only two people have won the World Cup as a player and as a coach. Germany's Franz Beckenbauer won in 1974 as player and 1990 as coach. Mario Zagallo of Brazil won as a player in 1958 and 1962, and as coach in 1970.

GERMANY'S WORLD CUP RECORD*

Wins	4
Losing finals	4
Semi-finals	5
Appearances	18
Matches played	106
Wins	66
Total goals	224

*up to and including 2014

GOALSCORING RECORDS

The World Cup's first goal was scored by Lucien Laurent of France, on 13 July 1930. The match had been going on for 19 minutes. Ever since, the world's best players have been trying to break World Cup scoring records.

Youngest …
The youngest scorer at the World Cup is Brazil's Pelé, who was 17 years and 239 days old when he scored against Wales in 1958. Pelé is also the youngest player to play in a final, at 17 years, 249 days. (The youngest player at a World Cup is Norman Whiteside of Northern Ireland, who was just 17 and 41 days when he played in 1982.)

… and oldest
Roger Milla of Cameroon was 42 years, 39 days old at the 1994 tournament. At the time, he was the oldest footballer ever at a World Cup. Milla scored in a match against Russia, making him the World Cup's oldest-ever goalscorer.

In 2018 Essam El-Hadary, Egypt's goalkeeper, became the oldest player ever to take part in a World Cup. He was 45 years and 161 days old.

Roger Milla of Cameroon (left), who played his last World Cup match at 42, shows a surprising turn of speed!

Fastest goal

Turkey scored the fastest World Cup goal ever against South Korea in 2002. Hakan Şükür hit the back of the net after just 11 seconds. Turkey finally won 3–2, which meant they finished third overall at only the second World Cup they ever played in.

Hakan Şükür, scorer of the fastest goal ever in a World Cup match, scores for Turkey at the 2002 World Cup. Şükür had a brilliant record in club football, too. Only once in 13 seasons did he score fewer than 10 goals.

Miroslav Klose (below, right) at the final of the 2014 World Cup, where he became the player with most World Cup goals. Klose scored at the 2002, 2006, 2010 and 2014 tournaments.

Most goals

4th: At the 1958 World Cup, Just Fontaine of France scored 13 goals … in only SIX matches. No one has ever scored more goals at a single World Cup. Fontaine did not play at another World Cup, which makes it amazing that he is fourth on the list of World Cup goal-scorers.

3rd: Gerd Müller of Germany (14 goals in 13 matches/two World Cups).

2nd: Ronaldo of Brazil (15 goals in 19 matches/four World Cups).

1st: Miroslav Klose of Germany (16 goals in 24 matches/four World Cups).

IT'S A FACT!

Ernest Wilimowski of Poland has the best goals-per-game average at the World Cup, with four per game. This isn't as impressive as it sounds: he played in only one game, and scored four goals. Next on the list are Sandor Kocsis of Hungary (average 2.2, 11 goals in 5 games) and Just Fontaine of France (average 2.2, 13 goals in 6 games).

THE 2022 WORLD CUP

21 November 2022: the 22nd Football World Cup kicks off in Qatar at 13:00. Across the globe, fans have set their clocks to Qatari time, so they don't miss a minute of the action ...

(1) AL BAYT
The design of this stadium is based on a traditional tent, used by nomads from the area.
Capacity: **60,000**

(2) LUSAIL ICONIC
The largest stadium, built to hold the final.
Capacity: **80,000**

(3) AL RAYYAN
Its design was inspired by the desert that surrounds it.
Capacity: **40,000**

(4) QATAR FOUNDATION
Also known as Education City Stadium as it is close to many of Doha's universities.
Capacity: **45,350**

THE WORLD CUP KICKS OFF
The 2022 World Cup starts at 13:00 on 21 November, at the Al Bayt Stadium in Al Khor City. The competition ends 27 days later, on Sunday 18 December, at Doha's Lusail Stadium. By then, the two teams left will have played six matches at the World Cup. One more win, and they will be world champions.

Most games at the 2022 World Cup will be played in and around Qatar's capital city, Doha.

RECORD SETTER!

The 2014 and 1998 World Cups are tied for the most goals scored in the tournament, with 171. The organisers of Qatar 2022 hoped that their competition would break the record.

Another record Qatar was aiming to beat was for the most people to have watched a live match. In Brazil in 2014, 3,386,810 people in total saw a match, and the average crowd per match was 52,918. Another World Cup was even more popular, though. At USA 1994, a total of 3,587,538 people watched matches — and because there were fewer games, the average crowd size was 68,991!

Huge crowds at Brazil 2014.

TRAVEL TIMES

At the 2018 World Cup in Russia, many teams had to fly long distances between matches. Qatar is a relatively small country, and every 2022 World Cup stadium is close to Doha. This made travel by coach possible for the teams. A new metro train system was also built to help fans travel to their team's matches.

HOT CONDITIONS

Even in winter, temperatures in Qatar can reach the mid-30s °C and the average temperature is about 27°C. To combat the heat, every stadium has a specially designed air-cooling system. These can reduce the temperature inside by over 10°C.

Possibly the world's only statue commemorating a head butt: the one that got Zinedine Zidane of France sent off during the 2006 World Cup Final (see below).

NO WAY!

In the first-ever World Cup final, Uruguay played Argentina. Thousands of Argentina fans had tickets, but missed the game — the riverboats bringing them to the match got lost in thick fog! Uruguay won 4-2.

RECORD SETTER!

Worst discipline at the World Cup? Zinedine Zidane of France, with four yellows and two reds — including one in the 110th minute of the 2006 final.

PLAYERS TO WATCH

If the worst player at the World Cup turned up at your local park, he would score goals whenever he wanted, and tackle everyone off the park. At the World Cup, though, it takes a *REALLY* special player to stand out. Here are ten of them.

LIONEL MESSI
Country: Argentina
Club: Paris St-Germain
Age at Qatar 2022: 35

If he plays, this will be Messi's last World Cup. Messi may be the world's best footballer: he has won the Ballon d'Or, the prize for the best player, seven times.

Messi has also won Europe's Golden Shoe for the best player in Europe six times, and the Champions' League four times. But he has not won the World Cup – yet.

HARRY KANE
Country: England
Club: Tottenham Hotspur
Age at Qatar 2022: 29

Kane had a tricky start to the 2021–22 season, after trying to leave Tottenham in the summer of 2021. However, England's captain is a deadly finisher when playing well (which he usually is) and won the prestigious Golden Boot at the World Cup in Russia in 2018.

Kane is also a popular, experienced team captain and will help England's younger star footballers play their best at the 2022 World Cup.

KEVIN DE BRUYNE
Country: Belgium
Club: Manchester City
Age at Qatar 2022: 31

Is de Bruyne the world's best midfielder? Maybe. His combination of passing ability (he can thread passes through gaps other players don't even see), long-range shots and free kicks can leave watchers open mouthed.

Belgium have a mix of experience and youth in their World Cup squad, and if de Bruyne is playing well they could go far in Qatar.

CHRISTIAN PULISIC
Country: USA
Club: Chelsea
Age at Qatar 2022: 24

Pulisic is sometimes nicknamed 'Captain America'. In a star-studded Chelsea team, Pulisic gets less playing time than he would like.

The USA will hope this means their lightning-quick winger is fresh for the World Cup in Qatar. Football fans everywhere will hope for the sight of Pulisic zipping past some of the world's best defenders!

THOMAS MÜLLER
Country: Germany
Club: Bayern Munich
Age at Qatar 2022: 33

Müller can play as an attacking midfielder, a second striker, a centre forward or on either wing.

He has always looked a little ungainly, and at 33 Müller will be a long way from the fastest player at the World Cup. But his special skill is finding space on the pitch that is not being defended – either for himself or whoever he is passing to – and that is unlikely to disappear because of his age.

Christian Pulisic

Neymar

Virgil Van dijk

NEYMAR
Country: Brazil
Club: Paris St-Germain
Age at Qatar 2022: 30

Brazil's second-highest goalscorer behind the legendary Pelé, Neymar played his first match as a professional at 17. He has been playing for Brazil since he was 18, and for most of that time has been one of the world's top strikers.

By the time Brazil qualified for Qatar, Neymar had scored 70 goals in 116 international matches: one of the best records in football.

KYLIAN MBAPPÉ
Country: France
Club: Paris St-Germain
Age at Qatar 2022: 23

Mbappé was only 19 when he played in the 2018 World Cup final and scored the match's best goal. Today his ability to dribble and terrifying turns of speed have the world's best defenders calling for their mummy!

Add to that Mbappé's goalscoring talent and it is no wonder he is seen as one of the world's best and most exciting players.

VIRGIL VAN DIJK
Country: Netherlands
Club: Liverpool
Age at Qatar 2022: 31

At 1.93 metres tall, van Dijk will be one of the tallest players at the World Cup. He is one of the world's best defenders, but van Dijk also scores goals – particularly from corners and free kicks.

A natural leader, van Dijk could help keep the Netherlands team – which in the past has suffered from a lack of unity – playing well together.

SERGEJ MILINKOVIC-SAVIC
Country: Serbia
Club: Lazio
Age at Qatar 2022: 27

Usually known as just Sergej (pronounced sir-gey), he has a pro-footballer dad and a pro-basketball-player mum. A versatile midfielder, Sergej can keep possession of the ball as teammates move forward, lead attacks and break up opposition moves.

At 1.91 metres tall Sergej is a big presence in a Serbian team loaded with stars.

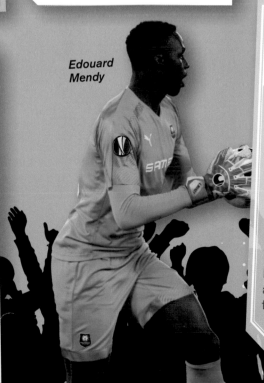

Edouard Mendy

EDOUARD MENDY
Country: Senegal
Club: Chelsea
Age at Qatar 2022: 30

Mendy got here the hard way. In 2014 he was unemployed and unable to find a job in football. At the last minute he was signed by Marseille, and after playing for several French clubs he moved to Chelsea, won the Champions League and became a star.

If Senegal are to do well, they will need Mendy (and defender Kalidou Koulibaly) to stop goals – and Sadio Mané to score them at the other end.

TOP TEAMS: ITALY

If Italy play well at the World Cup, the team often goes on to win. But unlike Brazil and Germany, Italy cannot be counted on to reach the semi-finals. In fact, as fans discovered in 2017 and again in 2022, they cannot be counted on even to qualify.

Famous matches

Italy has played in two of the most famous matches in World Cup history.

• In 1970, Italy beat Germany 4–3 in a semi-final game known as 'the Match of the Century'. The lead changed hands several times, and one German player was on the field with his arm in a sling, when Italy finally scored the winner in the 111th minute.

• In 1982, Italy's match against Brazil had everyone watching from the edges of their seats. Italy needed to win to carry on in the World Cup; Brazil could get through with a draw. Twice the famous Italy striker Paolo Rossi scored, giving Italy the lead. Twice the Brazilians scored in reply. Then, in the 74th minute, Rossi scored again: a **hat trick**! Italy was through – and went on to win the 1982 World Cup.

Italy's most recent win was in 2006, when the team beat Germany in the semi-final and France in the final.

Italy's first World Cup wins were in 1934 and 1938 (this photo shows the 1934 team). It would be over 40 years before they won the trophy again.

RECORD SETTER!
The latest goal ever in a World Cup match was scored in 2006. Italy's Alessandro del Piero hit the back of the net after 121 minutes of play: 90 minutes of normal time, 30 minutes of extra time, and one minute of injury time.

Mario Balotelli scores against England at the 2014 World Cup. It was the first game of the tournament for both teams. Italy eventually won 2–1.

Lightning strikes twice

There is an old saying that lightning (meaning disaster) doesn't strike twice. Italy fans would disagree. In 2017 they were plunged into despair when – for the first time since 1958 – Italy did not qualify for the World Cup. Never mind: they could look forward to the 2022 tournament – except… it happened again, when Italy were beaten in qualifying by lowly North Macedonia..

ITALY'S WORLD CUP RECORD*

Wins	4
Losing finals	2
Semi-finals	2
Appearances	18
Matches played	83
Wins	45
Total goals	128

*up to and including 2014

THE WORLD CUP'S BIGGEST FLOPS

The World Cup features the world's top players – but despite all the great footballers hanging around, there have been some terrible World Cup flops:

USA versus England, 1950

In 1950, the English were hot favourites to win. They had never played at a World Cup before, but they HAD recently beaten holders Italy 4–0 and Portugal 10–0. The USA team, meanwhile, had lost its last seven matches.

It must have come as a terrible shock to England to lose 1–0.

They never really recovered, and failed to get out of their group – for the first time, but not the last.

Joe Gaetjens of the USA slots the ball past England goalkeeper Bert Williams.

North Korea versus Italy, 1966

North Korea began the 1966 World Cup as 1,000-to-1 outsiders. Italy were among the favourites to win. Yet somehow, in the last game of their group, Korea managed a 1–0 win. Italy went home, and the Koreans were in the next round. There, after leading 3–0 at one point, they were knocked out 3–5 by Portugal.

Pak Doo-Ik scoring the winning goal against Italy.

France, 2002

As 1998 champions, France were expected to be fighting for the 2002 title. That didn't happen. They lost the first game, against Senegal. Then they drew 0–0 with Uruguay. And in their final game, against Denmark, France lost 2–0. The champions went home, without even scoring a single goal.

The fans' puffed-out cheeks and gloomy expressions say it all: France crash out of the 2002 World Cup.

THE WORST PENALTY MISSES

Even the best players sometimes find the pressure of taking a penalty too much. Here are four World Cup howlers:

1 *Roberto Baggio (right), 1994*
Baggio was one of the world's top players. When the World Cup final went to penalties, everyone expected him to slot the ball home. Unfortunately …

… Baggio hit it WAY over the crossbar, and Brazil won the World Cup.

2 *Stuart Pearce and Chris Waddle, 1990*
England and Germany were 1–1 at the end of extra time in the semi-final. After three penalties it was 3–3. Pearce had England's fourth penalty saved, and Germany scored theirs. Waddle had to score to keep England in it …

… but he hoofed the ball wide of the net. Germany went on to win the World Cup.

3 *Paul Ince and David Batty, 1998*
When the match against Argentina was a draw after extra time, England fans feared the worst. Ince's attempt was saved, and so was one of Argentina's. The score was 4–3 to Argentina – David Batty's kick had to go in …

… but Argentina's keeper stopped it. Argentina won, but were knocked out by the Netherlands at the next stage.

4 *Michel Platini (left), 1986*
Platini was one of the greatest French goal-scorers, and won the Ballon d'Or for the world's best player three times. In the 1986 quarter-final against Brazil, when the game ended in a penalty shootout, every France fan expected Platini to hit the net again. Except …

… he missed the goal by about a kilometre. It was a shocker, but at least Platini's was the only French miss. They won the shootout 4–3.

WORLD CUP AWARDS

At each World Cup finals, awards are given for the best performances in different areas of the game. These are some of the key ones:

The Golden Ball

The Golden Ball award is for the best player at the tournament. It is chosen from a list made up by FIFA. The world's media (the sports journalists who gather to watch the competition) decide on the winner. No one has ever won the Golden Ball more than once.

2018 winner: Luka Modric (Croatia)

Golden Boot

The Golden Boot is given to the player who scores the most goals. This award used to be called the Golden Shoe, but – possibly because 'golden shoe' sounded a bit silly – the name was changed in 2010.

2018 winner: Harry Kane (England) with six goals

Golden Glove

The Golden Glove is for the best goalkeeper at the World Cup. Even though they have their own special award, goalies can also win the Golden Ball. Only one player has ever managed this, though: Oliver Kahn of Germany, who won both in 2002.

2018 winner: Thibaut Courtois (Belgium)

Man of the Match and Best Young Player

These are awards the public can vote for, via the FIFA website. Man of the Match awards go to the players people think were the best footballer in the best games of the tournament. The Best Young Player is for players who are 21 or less during the World Cup.

2018 winners:
Antoine Griezmann (France)
and Kylian Mbappé (France)

Kylian Mbappé shows off the skills that secured him joint Best Young Player at the 2018 World Cup.

Antoine Griezmann in action for the French team.

Fair Play Trophy

This trophy is given to the team with the best ranking for fair play, according to FIFA's regulations. To win, your team has to collect as few yellow and red cards as possible. Only teams that make it to the knockout stages are eligible.

2018 winners: Spain (below)

WINNING TEAMS AND BEATEN FINALISTS

Year	Winner	Second place	Host country
1930	Uruguay	Argentina	Uruguay
1934	Italy	Czechoslovakia	Italy
1938	Italy	Hungary	France
1950	Uruguay	Brazil	Brazil
1954	West Germany*	Hungary	Switzerland
1958	Brazil	Sweden	Sweden
1962	Brazil	Czechoslovakia	Chile
1966	England	West Germany	England
1970	Brazil	Italy	Mexico
1974	West Germany	The Netherlands	West Germany
1978	Argentina	The Netherlands	Argentina
1982	Italy	West Germany	Spain
1986	Argentina	West Germany	Mexico
1990	West Germany	Argentina	Italy
1994	Brazil	Italy	USA
1998	France	Brazil	France
2002	Brazil	Germany	South Korea and Japan
2006	Italy	France	Germany
2010	Spain	The Netherlands	South Africa
2014	Germany	Argentina	Brazil
2018	France	Croatia	Russia

* western part of Germany, which from 1949 to 1990 was a separate country

FINDING OUT MORE

PLACES TO VISIT

FIFA World Football Museum
Seestrasse 27
8002 Zurich
Switzerland

It's probably too far for a school trip … but if you ever happen to be in Zurich, Switzerland, FIFA's football museum is well worth a visit. Among the permanent exhibitions here is one about the World Cup; there are also exhibits about the women's World Cup, the history of football and some amazing photos linked to the game.

The museum also has a great website at: www.fifamuseum.com

The National Football Museum
Urbis Building
Cathedral Gardens
Manchester M4 3BG
England

Confidently claiming to be 'the world's biggest and best football museum', the museum tours are great not only for fanatical fans, but also those who are less-than-mad about the game. The varied exhibits include the birth of football in England, England's 1966 World Cup win and even football-related art.

The museum has an interesting website at: www.nationalfootballmuseum.com

THE INTERNET

As you would expect, many of the World Cup's most famous moments are available to watch online:

Geoff Hurst's 1966 'goal' for England – was it? Wasn't it? Judge for yourself in this colourised clip:
http://tinyurl.com/jgvhwy7

If you like the drama of a penalty shootout, try this one for size: Italy versus France, 2006. The tension is incredible:
http://tinyurl.com/z5qlazp

Brazil's top World Cup goals:
http://tinyurl.com/hx7sb7l

FIFA videos of the ten best goals at the last two World Cups:
2014: http://tinyurl.com/hgwfnyj
2010: http://tinyurl.com/hg699oa

This collection of ten scorching goals from the Women's World Cup in 2015 shows that women's football is just as skilful and exciting as the men's game:
http://tinyurl.com/zfjuz6d

Note to parents and teachers: Every effort has been made by the Publishers to ensure that these websites are suitable for children, that they are of the highest educational value, and that they contain no inappropriate or offensive material. However, because of the nature of the Internet, it is impossible to guarantee that the contents of these sites will not be altered. We strongly advise that Internet access is supervised by a responsible adult.

GLOSSARY

amateur *unpaid*

break *attack made suddenly, after breaking up the other team's attack by grabbing possession*

CONCACAF *short for Confederation of North, Central American and Caribbean Association Football*

Czechoslovakia *European country that became the Czech Republic and Slovakia in 1993*

disallowed *removed from the scoreboard*

dribble *run with the ball close to your feet, regularly giving it little kicks ahead*

eligible *able to enter or be included*

FIFA *short for Fédération Internationale de Football Association, the organisation in charge of world football*

hat trick *three goals by the same player in one match*

host nation *country where an international event is held*

nutmegging *play the ball through the legs of an opponent*

open play *normal play – not periods of stoppage such as a free kick or corner*

penalty shootout *way of deciding the winner of a football match if the scores are equal after extra time. Each team takes five penalties, and the one with most goals wins. If the result is still a tie, the teams keep taking penalties until there is a winner*

possession *in football, possession means your team having the ball*

professional *paid*

red card *card shown to a player to signal that they are being sent off*

statistic *fact gained from looking at numbers*

yellow card *card shown to a player for a bad offence. Two yellows results in being sent off*

INDEX